# BULLS**T BRILLIANCE

The #1 undisputed source in creating awesome crap to get yourself out of trouble

Joel S. Levinson

**Bulls\*\*t Brilliance: The #1 undisputed source in creating awesome crap to get yourself out of trouble**

Copyright © 2017 by Joel S. Levinson.

Published by Live The Risk, LLC. Phoenix, AZ

www.BSBrilliance.com
www.LiveTheRisk.com

First Edition.    ISBN-10: 0-9911841-1-4
　　　　　　　　ISBN-13: 978-0-9911841-1-8

All rights reserved. No part of this publication may be copied, reproduced or utilized in any form or by any means, including electronic, mechanical, photocopying, recording, or by information storage retrieval system, without prior permission of the author. For information about permission to reproduce selections from this book, write to support@BSBrilliance.com

This book is presented for informational purposes only. No legally protected advice, including legal, financial, tax, spiritual, personal, relationship or bull raising, is provided or intended. Use with sound judgment and at your own risk.

Readers should be aware that internet websites offered as citations or sources for further information may have changed or disappeared between the times this was written and when read.

The information presented herein represents the views of the author as of the date of publication. Due to the rate at which conditions change, the author reserves the right to alter and update his opinions at any time. While every attempt has been made to verify the information in this book, the author does not assume any responsibility for errors, inaccuracies or omissions. And just to make it clear, the author is calling all bullshit, bullshit.

Limit of Liability/Disclaimer of Warranty: While the publisher and author have used their best efforts in preparing this book, they make no representations or warranties with respect to the accuracy or completeness of the contents of this book and specifically disclaim any implied warranties of merchantability or fitness for a particular purpose. No warranty may be created or extended by sales representatives or written sales materials.

The advice and strategies contained herein may not be suitable for your situation. Consult with a professional where appropriate. Neither the publisher nor author shall be liable for any loss of profit or any other commercial or personal damages, including but not limited to special, incidental, consequential, or other damages. They also take no responsibilities that this book is appropriate for anyone of any age. They expect none of the contents of this book to actually work.

Just in case you are wondering, the "#1 undisputed source" from the cover is also bullshit.

| | |
|---|---|
| Book Launch: | Karin Olson, Esq. (www.KarinOlson.com) |
| Final Polish: | KM Creative Design (kmcreative2323@earthlink.net) |
| Editing: | Horizon Rose Editing (http://www.horizonroseediting.co.vu) |
| Cover & Layout: | Expanding Star, Inc. |
| Images licensed: | iStock.com/uisp65 & briefcase image © Graphics Factory.com |

**Dedicated to all of my friends and family who have called me on my bullshit.**

**Thanks for helping me improve!**

## *Thank you*

Without my wife, Jackie and my daughters, Jaime and Sarah, there would be no reason to write this book (or any book). They listen to my bullshit all of the time and give me the energy to accomplish the impossible anyway.

I can't thank my Live The Risk business partner, friend, and brother, Jeff Steele, enough for agreeing to and supporting the anti-adaptation of the awesome material we created in our first book, *Live The Risk,* to fuel the education, fun and sarcasm of this book. Without his help, I would have actually had to research the contents of bullshitting, and that just sounded like a lot of work.

An outrageously big thanks to Karin Olson for without her help this bullshit of a book would have never even gotten out of my computer and on to the charts.

Without a final once-over from the talented Kari MaKenna, this bullshit might not have sounded as good as it could have. Many thanks, Sis; you're the best!

An enormous hug to Callan Rush, Justin Livingston, Nancy Juetten, and Kate Harlow for their continued support as I better my shit from stage.

A giant thank you to Nola Yergen, Nadine Smigla Zimmermann, Vasili Xiarhos, Laura Correia and Candace Stump for reading the early manuscripts and telling me that my bullshit needed to be more brilliant.

Also, a special thanks to all of the deflection collaborators; without their help, the list of excuses would have never been created:

Deborah Woods, Louie Cornay, Rick Tilley, Charlie Thoj, Paul St.John, Robert Miller, Tanner Miller, Kaeleigh Lamb, Charlie Hunzinger, Carol Ragusa, Lisa M Boggs, Paul Christ, Britnee Ruscitti Kenyon, Brandi Weaver, Gwen Simshauser, Jodi Levinson Hardiek, Brian Lapham, Ian Zimmermann, Brandon Zimmermann, Jadyn Zimmermann, Tanner Simpson, Rudy McCarthy, Laura Correia, Charles E. Davis, Jennifer Greene Lutes, Alicia Spallas, Karen Sue Fromm, Tracie Kudamatsu Aillie, Jim Heronime, Judith Cobb, Laura Tilley Mesner, Teresa Felder, Stacy Deprey-Purper, Nicole Jones, Misty O'Brien Stachel, Mark Alva and Jacob Meade.

Btw, just because the collaborators are listed above doesn't mean they condone, appreciate or use the word bullshit, anything that means bullshit, or making excuses that are represented in this manuscript. In fact, I totally expect that they don't.

# TABLE OF CONTENTS

The Backward Foreword ............................................................ 11

The Best Way To Achieve Less Is To Bullshit More ..................... 15

The World Expects Bullshit ....................................................... 18

The Rubber Meets The Road When The Bullshit Hits The Fan .... 22

Ancient Greek Bullshit .............................................................. 31

The Bullshit Bullprint ................................................................ 40

Many Paths To Bullshit Brilliance .............................................. 56

Justification Bullshit ................................................................. 65

Ugliness Bullshit ....................................................................... 74

Defensive Bullshit ..................................................................... 83

Gratification Bullshit ................................................................. 92

Entitlement Bullshit .................................................................. 98

Real Examples of Bullshit Brilliance ......................................... 102

Better Bullshit Than The Bullshitter That Is Bullshitting You ..... 106

Never Deliver Borderline Bullshit ............................................. 115

Sometimes Skitsnack Is Just Paskapuhe .................................. 121

About The Author .................................................................... 125

About Live The Risk ................................................................. 127

# The Backward Foreword

So, I wanted to help write this book, but holy moly there was always - and I mean *always* - something else to get done. Where do I begin? How about the new puppy? He needs constant attention. In fact, he ate one pair of shoes while I typed the last line. Seriously.

Then there are the never-ending house chores. It feels like I get two things crossed off the list and five more are added. It never fails. As I get something cleaned the kids and pets are right behind me in a tornado of dust and dirt. I am always exhausted.

The yard looks like it was used for an autocross death race and there were no survivors . . . my plants and trees were the victims. It's already bad enough that I don't have a green thumb, but to hear the neighbors talk you'd think our house was the worst on the entire block. They may be right.

And don't even get me started on the dire situation in the garage. Actually, to call it a garage isn't accurate, since we've never parked a car in there the entire time we've lived in the house. Yeah, it looks like I'm hoarding, and . . . well . . . I just might be.

Speaking of the car, when was the last time that it got washed? I think Jefferson was still president.

What about the bills? The constant bills. The never-ending bills. I'm up to my neck in bills. Of course, they have to get paid . . . or do they? Okay, yes, they must be paid, and that usually means more time at work to make money to pay those endless bills.

And I just love being at work because I have nothing else I'd rather be doing. Work always takes center stage. I have to schedule my week, month and life around work. I can't even take time off without permission. Basically, it's work's fault that I can't get my personal act together. Or is it the fault of the bills . . . which are why I must work. Heck yeah, it's their fault. The both of them. I'm just a pawn.

The last time I was on time to anything . . . was most likely never. I just can't get going in the mornings, and I can't settle down in the evenings. I feel like I'm running a race, and every single time I near the finish line it gets moved another 100 yards away. It's not my fault that my life is in constant turmoil. It is what it is and it has nothing to do with me. Call it fate. Actually, that's a great idea - let's say it's fate's fault.

What about the family? Oh yeah, those people who live in the house with me. Our house has a revolving door for a reason. Between sports, extracurricular activities, parent-teacher meetings, and homework, it's a wonder that I even know what they look like. And when was the last time I went on a date with my lovely wife? Usually we're running in opposite directions for work or groceries or kids or chores. We last went on a real date several years ago, and I haven't seen her since.

Here's the truth: There's always going to be something that gets in the way . . . and if you don't apply what Joel talks about within these pages, it is going to be held against you. Housework. Homework. Chores. Events. Conferences. Work. Meetings. Games. Puppies. Bills. Appointments. Follow his instructions and get a good pile, round it out, and throw before anybody sees you.

Everyone gets 24 hours in a day - the difference is in how each person spends his/her most precious asset, time. That's the key and always has been. Use your time wisely to create the bullshit you need... or don't.

~ Jeff Steele

# Chapter One:
# The Best Way To Achieve Less Is To Bullshit More

Here you go: the book that no one wants me to write because the truth will be revealed to all.

Finally, some education on the wonderful world of bullshit.

Now, I'm not talking about just ordinary *dëngla*[1]. I'm talking about the stuff that makes any conversation smell better, the kind of stuff that others will be in awe of; yep, I'm talking about the cream of the crop of inserting bullshit into conversations.

I'm determined to blow the lid off this steaming subject!

As you know, there are many types of bullshit. There is the kind that embellishes a story: if you think of any movie or book, it's bullshit. Most of the characters aren't real, the settings have been embellished, the interactions altered, and no matter how beautiful, horrific, or sexual the story, you know that there is some extraneous excrement somewhere.

---

[1] *Dëngla* is Albanian bullshit

Then there is the type of bullshit that expands on your activities or credentials - exaggerations and assumptions (just think of your teenage years or any politician).

**Finally, there's the bullshit that this book is about - excuse creation.**

Because in today's day and age, you need to be ready to give the world your best self-preservation phrases because that is what great excuses are when delivered with grace and aplomb. Your brilliance will ensure you remain comfortable AND have a way out. No doubt, a great excuse delivered correctly will keep your record clean by avoiding blame and guilt.

The bullshit in this book is about developing, creating and delivering awesome-sounding phrases that have the capability to get you out of trouble. In other words, filler words to misdirect, alter, excuse or deflect the receiver of your prose. You are going to learn what it's going to take to make any audience – be it wife, husband, child, friend, boss, dad, mom, doctor, police officer or bank cashier – appreciative and understanding of why you didn't do what you said you'd do.

What better bullshit is there?

I get it; you're probably telling yourself that you've been bullshitting your way out of trouble for most of your life - how will a book help you improve yours? Why read these pages to help you develop, construct and deliver your excuses better than you ever have? Why learn the differences between poor excuses and brilliant bullshit?

Honestly, if you don't learn, someone else will. And your friends, family and co-workers will use their extraordinary excrement experiences against you.

And I believe if anyone should use bullshit to create selective amnesia in the receiver, especially so one no longer worries about what you were going to do, it should be you, the reader, who took the time to master your own shit.

And it's my mission to help you find the fun in stretching your BS muscle to dominate your dëngla!

# Chapter Two:
# The World Expects Bullshit

I'm not asking you to take a leap of faith in developing, constructing and delivering a great excuse. You're just fulfilling what you were taught to do and, believe it or not, *encouraged* to do.

Wild claim? I think not.

My proof: from birth, parents whom I admire and appreciate train their kids to develop good excuses by asking the most infamous simple question of all time (which they know their children don't have a real answer for).

The question that starts the training at such a young age is the same one that cements the knowledge in the child's mind that great excuses can get them out of trouble:

*"Why did you do that?"*

For example:

> *Parent:* *Did you knock over the flour onto the kitchen floor? Why did you do that?*
> *Kid:* *It wasn't me. It was my invisible friend.*
> *Parent:* *<starts to clean up as they laugh>*
>
> *Parent:* *Did you give the dog a bath in the toilet? Why did you do that?*
> *Kid:* *It wasn't me. He jumped in; I was saving him. And yes, the soap also fell in.*
> *Parent:* *<laughs and gets a towel to dry the dog>*

Indeed, your parents wanted you to bullshit; they just didn't want you to learn that naughty word. Heck, they put poo on parade all of the time for you to learn from – Santa and the Easter Bunny are some of the best BS the world has ever known.

Parents aren't alone in this transmission of turd training:

- Society has made it a norm, a global expectation, that you better have an excuse, a damn good excuse, that they can interpret as a reason for not doing something you promised - and it better be better than good. I couldn't come up with a more perfect value proposition for this book;

- Schools train students to create reasons (aka excuses) for why they didn't get something done;

- Employers require excuses for not only why stuff doesn't get done but also why we call to take a day off from work, need to leave early or do just about anything.

The world has made it *appropriate* behavior, and, even better, *acceptable* behavior, to apply the principles of bullshit brilliance. I guess that is why everyone is doing it, not just kids - adults, executives, politicians, lawyers, doctors, accountants, teachers, employers and employees. The truth is, everyone is full of shit and I'm just here to help you get the most out of it when used in conjunction with excusing yourself from expected behaviors.

So here it is. If you are going to use excuses, if you are going to fling it, then why not be the best? Show pride in your ability to manipulate and connive your way out of personal responsibility.

In the end, why feel the guilt of not doing your chores? Why process that emotion? Heck, why do the homework assigned? Why be ready to go at a time that you said? Why be to an event at the time you promised?

Sooner or later, the chores will get done with or without you. What's the difference if the homework gets done? Is it going to help you? No doubt the world will still revolve if you are 10 minutes late or never arrive. Of course, it might not just be chores, homework, or being late that matters. It might be that you want to protect the most valuable and misguided perception that you have - your ego.

Heck, your bullshit might help you from doing a job that is below your pay grade. Maybe this one thing that needs to get done just isn't your cup of tea, and you want to let the boss down easy; as we all know, a bad excuse can't do that, only brilliant bullshit can.

This is why having your brilliance ready and waiting might protect you from showing your inadequacies, vulnerabilities, or maybe even your foolishness (that is, if you have any - and most great deflectors don't.) Because you know that the only thing that matters is that they understand your carefully crafted words and ignore your actions, because, like sheep, they are easily led.

A genuine hope of using the content of this book is that you will discover what bullshit is and what it isn't.

# Chapter Three:

# The Rubber Meets The Road When The Bullshit Hits The Fan

Here is where the rubber meets the road - to make sure that when you fling those nuggets of goodness, they're going to stick. You don't want anything that is going to hit the fan and then splatter back. You should be expecting to have it affix where you want it and nowhere else. Yep, your carefully crafted deflection needs to have laser-like accuracy.

Of course, to have that happen, you can't do what most have done. You can't leverage the uncreative poo we provided as kids, alter them with better adult-sounding words, and then re-use them as adults. It just won't do anymore.

Honestly, "The dog ate my homework" isn't good enough to achieve the desired results because if you use your standard kid shit every time you don't want to do something, it's going to get old, stale and dried-out. No one is going to believe you. No one is going to judge you not guilty. It becomes nothing more than the boy who cried wolf. And crying wolf is for getting attention.

**Keep in mind, bullshit brilliance is about removing focus from what you didn't get done, not gaining it.**

Back to the words you use. I get it; you like your shit and don't want to let it go. Without the appropriate rules of good deflections to avoid commitments - how should I say this politely - they aren't going to work!

You have the right to get out of what you committed to do. If what you're saying isn't getting you out of that requirement, then what good were the words? Indeed, why fling the crap at someone and not have it hit its target? The words of a brilliant bullshitter need to razzle-dazzle and confuse the listener, but most importantly they need to free YOU from your missed obligation.

Your rights are well protected by *The Official and Unadulterated Bull of Rights* that all novice and professional bullshitters should live by. Your rights should not be ignored or enforced, but should continue to serve as a reminder that you have a right to bullshit when and where you deem necessary.

## The Official and Unadulterated Bull of Rights

*The Convention of a number of long-standing Bullshit throwers, sayers and other experts, having at the time of their adoption of this Bull Of Rights, express a desire, in order to prevent misconstruction or abuse of its bullshit, and to best ensure the beneficent ends of its institution, set forth the following:*

1. You have the right to make excuses.

2. You have the right to be judged not guilty.

3. You have the right to have any excuse you made not held against you in a court of law… or any other place… or by anybody else.

4. You have the right to be free and clear on any spoken or unspoken expectations – with or without the help of an attorney.

5. You have the right to construct and deliver bullshit in any creative way possible, so as to achieve the desired results.

6. The right and power to be secure and confident in your bullshit shall not be violated.

7. *You have the right to remain silent, to speak loudly and to waffle between the two whenever and wherever such serves you, and even when it doesn't, and there should be no making of any law or rules to prevent your free exercise of such.*

8. *You have the right to keep and bear bullshit and such right shall not be infringed.*

9. *You have the right to not care what others think as you deliver your bullshit in time of peace or war.*

10. *You have the right to avoid a speedy and impartial determination by fellow bullshitters of the fate of any of the bullshit you deliver.*

11. *Excessive penalty shall not be imposed, nor excessive requirements applied, nor shall cruel and unusual punishments be inflicted as a result of any bullshit you fling.*

12. *The enumerated rights in this Bull of Rights shall not be construed to deny or disparage any other bullshit you might seek to dish out.*

So, if you want to maintain your rights and be successful at removing that promise that you made – then let's get creative!

Let's take bullshitting and pile it up to the next level; let's put some science behind the deflection. Let's show some gumption and make it an AWESOME reason in the receiver's head for why you didn't do it, and have fun while not living up to your commitments. Think of it as a game of "Catch me if you can." Or, better yet, "I didn't do it, and you're not going to do anything about it. Ha!"

I'm sure you have these thoughts in your head: "I don't need an excuse not to do something," "I'm an adult," or the best deflection to not do something if you are under 18: "I'm just a kid." Excuses are like bungholes: everybody has one, so your deflection is going to need to be a standout. Yep, you are going to need to be the best ass in the room, and in the end, the best ass among asses.

Let's regress a little and go back to the "kid" reason. The reason I said it was the best excuse is that it works, and other children understand it. And if they were you, they weren't planning on doing it either. Even adults expect it because they were once kids too. Now, don't get me wrong, adults will attempt to leverage their years (a lot of years) of experience to tell you "if I only knew then what I know now." That is just their attempt to fling some dung for why they didn't do what they said they were going to when they were your age.

As for the adult bullshit, it's immediately understood by all other adults. Other adults know the pressures that *adulting* can bring. They understand the inflexibility, time constraints and harsh expectations. They appreciate your crap about why you won't get what you promised done. And when the kids listen to your excuse, they will store it away for future use - remember, we train our children to bullshit.

The more I think and write about this subject, the more I understand that there's nothing like a great excuse to prevent you from accepting the negative consequences of your actions. Gotta love it!

Maybe it's time for an example of the result: Imagine for me if what you promised to your boss NEVER had to be delivered. How easy would your job become? Of course, now thinking about it, what if your boss read this same book and whatever he promised to you (e.g., a raise) was never delivered? Let's hope that he *has* read this book, and his excuse isn't weak at all. Actually, for the sake of your sanity, let's hope that his bullshit is better than great, let's hope it's BRILLIANT, because I don't want you hurt by someone not delivering a promise to you.

So now's the time to start cultivating the best list of deflections ever, because they will be the protection clauses that you invoke to keep out of trouble, to minimize the repercussions, and to eliminate the disappointment from others. And really, what's their frustration worth when compared to the time and effort you save to avoid the work? No comparison.

Though disappointments, repercussions and regrets are the tip of the iceberg, there are plenty of other problems that brilliant bullshit can help shield you from:

- It could be the unknown, not knowing the next step to take, the possible truth, or operating outside of your comfort zone. Each one plays with your head to the point that it scares you and you want to escape from your challenge. *Keep in mind: Fears aren't facts; they are your projected assumptions.* You're aware of the worst scenario happening (even though it hasn't) and you need to protect yourself from your future self's results because of what others might negatively say about you. I guess you could say that you have seen the future and it is crap.

- Maybe someone is forcing his or her method of work madness on you and you just don't want to work that hard. You know that it might get done one day, just not today, and hopefully not by you.

- You have come to a conclusion that enough is enough, and there is no reason to gain more skill to get the job done. Or you are tired of playing someone else's game and you want no one to judge you for what you have or haven't done. Or people in your work, home or play environments are always doing something to you. It's their fault, not yours. It's their crap. You have a right to protect yourself from them.

So in a nutshell, the rest of this book is about letting me make this bullshitting thing as easy as possible for you. Because no matter what is going on in your life that requires an excuse to be built and delivered, you need to make sure that your crap is grade A.

You are on the verge of having the listeners of your verbal *ordure*[2] commend you for your creative genius and forget what they wanted you to do. If done at the level expected, the receiver of your words will bask in the glory of your amazing phrase construction and will hold your ninja-like skills of deflection in high regard - and they won't even know that you did nothing more than construct a crap bouquet of doo-doo flowers.

I'm really excited for you to have this training. In fact, I have more waiting for you than could possibly fit in this book at www.BSBrilliance.com.

If you want your own personal copy of The Official and Unadulterated Bull of Rights just follow the link and I will send it straight to your email inbox for free:

www.BSBrilliance.com/BSB-1

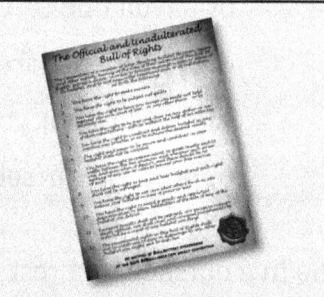

---

[2] *Ordure* is English for excrement

# Chapter Four:
# Ancient Greek Bullshit

Let me introduce the Greek goddess of excuses, *Prophasis* (pronounced *Prof'-as-is*). She is the daughter of the Titan Epimetheus, the god of afterthought (I guess this kind of crap runs in the family). I'm betting that few have heard of her, but Prophasis was just as impactful as any other Greek gods, maybe even more so, because her precepts, principles and pitfalls are used today when a deflection of a promise is delivered correctly. From what I discovered (mind you, I didn't dig too deep - at least that is my excuse) Prophasis gave these critical words to the world: "*Omilía den eínai fthiní - eínai doreán!*" or "Talk isn't cheap – it's free!"

Now, I should write paragraphs about Prophasis, how she came about in Greek mythology and why the connection to excuse and deflection was created. But if I research a lot for this book, it will set a standard for all of the other books that I am planning on writing, so I am going to pass. (Wouldn't you?) Plus the amount of time required to put it all down in writing and for you to read it, is well… a lot.

So for your sake I am not going to waste any more time other than to tell you that when you add up all of her information....

**You are here to understand and appreciate the science of doo and acquire the handiwork to develop, create and deploy the appropriate bullshit to remove the consequences of the actions you didn't take.**

Let's get into the Wayback Machine and reminisce that you, at one time or another, were using parts and pieces of Prophasis' Ratiology[3]. True, your parents didn't call it that, and you didn't know you were practicing that, but you were doing it - and for 96.3% of the kids out there, they were doing it as well. You didn't need no stinking book to tell you anything.

Let's stroll down memory lane and relive some of your childhood excuses. As you know, each one doesn't only work for when you want to get out of something. Sometimes you leveraged bull poopy to explain why you did something that you weren't supposed to. Come on this journey to your past and just think about the things you said while under the age

---

[3] *Ratio* is Latin for rationale, rationale is a synonym for excuse, and *ology* means any science or branch of knowledge. So, Ratiology is the science of excuses.

of 18 that saw the results that you are attempting to get now. Actually, just make a checkmark next to the ones that did work for you:

"I didn't get enough sleep."
*"I got too much sleep."*
"I'm too tired."
*"It wasn't me."*
"It was (insert name of sibling or pet)."
*"It isn't mine."*
"I didn't know."
"I asked you, and you said I could."
"I'm exhausted."
"I thought I heard you say it was ok."
"I'm feeling a huge amount of pressure, and this is just adding to it."
"I don't see how I can accomplish all these things."
"I need more time."
"I didn't have enough time."
"I have a headache."
"My (insert body part) hurts, and that will make it hurt more."
"That's not mine to clean up."
"I'm sick."
"They were sick."

*"It will make me sick."*

"It was an accident."

*"It wasn't my fault."*

"I was scared."

*"I was bored."*

"They hit me first!"

*"They started it."*

"It's just how I'm wired."

*"That's how they do it in other countries."*

"My friend came over."

*"I was gonna… BUT…"*

"This was all your fault, (insert relative or person who lives with you)."

*"Just a couple of more minutes (before doing anything else)."*

"They made me do it."

*"I didn't hear you."*

 "I can't. I'm busy."

*"I don't care."*

"I thought you said…"

*"I don't have any homework."*

"I already did it."

*"It isn't due yet."*

"I'm getting help on it tomorrow."

*"I didn't bring home the book."*

"I thought I had it in my backpack."

"Everyone else does it."

"My job isn't to get straight A's."

"You just want me to be perfect."

"No one reminded me."

"I'm not perfect."

"You didn't say please."

"No one told me."

"What are you talking about?"

"Shouldn't we just solve the problem first before I work on my weak points?"

"That's so insensitive. I can't believe you would bring THAT up."

"You just don't want to help me."

"I didn't mean to fall asleep."

"Do you want me to fail?"

"Do you want me to starve/puke/die/etc.?"

"It's not like I'm going to get it anyway."

"Not like you didn't do it when you were a kid."

"Yeah, yeah . . . I heard you the first time."

"I didn't see you there."

"I was getting to it."

"Time is just a number."

"I ran out of time."

"I thought that was the way you said to do it."

*"I don't respect that teacher."*

"That teacher doesn't respect me."

*"I'm never going to use that stuff in real life."*

"I wouldn't be a teen if I didn't try it once."

*"I was going to do it, but then you talked to me again."*

"It doesn't inspire me."

*"I wasn't there."*

"I didn't do my homework in that class because scholars don't do busy work."

*"I didn't want to tell you because you wouldn't understand."*

"Sorry, I was busy working on the other thing you told me to do."

*"I'm waiting for you to make lunch."*

"That's (insert sibling's name)'s job."

"I already did it... someone must have messed it up again."

"We should spend our time home relaxing, not working more."

*"I have to go to the bathroom."* (And then wait in there until the requestor leaves.)

"I didn't know what you wanted me to do next."

*"Sorry, I can't; I have my own stuff to do."*

"... but I PROMISE to do it tomorrow!!"

Of course, as an adult, some of your kid excuses might not transcend the trip to the work world, mainly because you're supposed to have the capability to motivate yourself. But if you think about it, isn't the work world just giving you their bullshit to convince you to get even more done than what they are paying you for? In either case, let's think about the excuses that you give as adulthood arrived:

"I didn't want to."
*"I wasn't in charge."*
"I don't understand your logic."
*"No, I'm not happy to see you."*
"I was doing something else."
*"Someone died."*
"I have jury duty."
*"I have to go to court."*
"My recent body cavity search has caused me to be shy around people."
*"I am/they are sick."*
"I need to stay home to care for my spouse/child/parent/pet."
*"I am distracted by something else."*
"I am annoyed by people."
*"I have a family/personal issue/emergency."*
"I stayed up late working and I am too tired to come in."

*"My alarm didn't go off."*

"Power went off in the middle of the night."

*"It's my birthday!"*

"I can't tell you; it's just too embarrassing."

*"Way too much food/alcohol/noise last night."*

"Need to wait for a delivery."

*"I had a situation to take care of."*

"I'm having an allergic reaction."

*"My ride didn't show up."*

"My phone is dead."

*"I need to stay close to the bathroom."* Followed up with, *"Do you really want to know?"*

"My doctor says that I need to stay home and rest."

*"My relationship is on the rocks and . . ."*

"I'm infectious and don't want to get anyone sick."

*"Something very embarrassing happened and . . ."*

"My car won't start/I locked my keys in the car/I got a flat and I am waiting to get it fixed."

*"I was in an accident."*

"I hurt my (insert body part)."

*"The dog/cat/rat/hamster/bird ran away/died/needs something."*

"You didn't know it, but today is a religious holiday for me."

*"I'm an introvert/extrovert."*

Now, each of the above well-crafted bundles has some meat on the bone; they aren't just filling space like the kids' excuses did. An adult conversation pile makes the receiver want to give up on the task he assigned you. Why? Because the words used are plausible, understandable, appreciated, and, most importantly, support Prophasis' precepts and principles and avoid her pitfalls.

So let's return to the present, put the Wayback Machine away, and focus on the future crap you're planning to sling by concentrating on a blueprint that will make everything you say look and smell better.

# Chapter Five:
# The Bullshit Bullprint

I am confident that if Prophasis was alive today, she would have leveraged her learnings to form the same Bullshit Blueprint, or should I say "No Trouble Bullprint," that I am about to share with you (even though it probably would have been written in Greek).

You can think of this bullprint as a one-stop shop for most of your bullshit needs. It is a culmination of Prophasis' precepts, principles and pitfalls plus words of wisdom that will hopefully keep you safe and sound from the activities that you are attempting to avoid.

So let's not waste any more words and jump right in to the architectural bullprint called bullshit:

**Precept #1: Keep it simple**

Your bullshit doesn't need to be complicated or complex. By keeping it simple you can improvise if necessary, although this is a skill best left to those with years of experience. Remember, *practice makes perfect*.

## Precept #2: Keep it real

Bullshit only works if the receiver believes it is authentic and understands it. She must see it as possible and genuine. (No fake shit for her. . . only the real doo-doo will do.) And if she has personally experienced what you are describing, it will contribute significantly to getting your crap accepted. Now, to improve the acceptance of the excuse to the receiver, it is important that you believe what you said - if you don't believe your BS, who will? If the receiver can appreciate your superior-sounding shit, you will have a leg up on completing your objective. It's your *hovadina*[4], and don't let anyone take it from you.

## Precept #3: Make sure your peeps understand

The biggest cause of disapproval of your bullshit is that what you have decided to use isn't appropriate for yourself. You don't have, as the youth of today would say, the "street cred" to have your crap believed. So save a significant amount of time, straining and energy by checking your work against your demographic group.

---

[4] *Hovadina* is Czech Bullshit

Your demographic group can be one or more of the following: age, gender, living arrangement (house, apartment, roommates), children (gender, age, number), animals (age, type, number, expected anger issues), job, car (age, type), race, creed, rank or responsibilities.

For example: A young employee can't say to their department manager, "I'm just not good with technology," because most likely the young person was raised on the internet and technology.

**Precept #4: Invoke sympathy and empathy**

Keep in mind the objective: you need your bullshit to stick to the receiver. If the receiver doesn't feel an emotional reaction, then chances are he won't care about what you've said. If done correctly, after saying your words, he will want to console and support you after delivering the biggest pile of your life.

The secret sauce to brilliance is to make your receiver know just what you mean when you offer heaping servings of it. Tap into something you know about him - for example, if he has a pet peeve about bad drivers, you can tell a story about how you were only late because a bad driver cut you off and caused you to miss the green light.

It is also entirely appropriate to use something that you know sparks his emotions, such as you were running on time until a dog (or cat depending on his preference) got hit by a car and you stopped to help; that one works great.

**Precept #5: Don't give too much detail**

Here is the lowdown to this rule: think before you squirt out your brilliant phrases. If you want the receiver to accept and appreciate what you have said, don't give too much detail. Details open you up to possible fact checking.

Think about the dog/cat getting hit by a car excuse. Keep it necessary. The dog had four legs and after it got hit it had three. See, just enough detail to make it real. You don't want so much detail that he begins to question some part of the excuse - I mean, reason.

## Precept #6: Change the subject quickly

Before the receiver can ask a ton of questions, quickly change the subject. The last thing you want to do is to play in the bullshit you put out. This step is critical. So, when he asks about the dog that got hit, say something along the lines of, "It was so upsetting. I don't understand how people can do such a thing." Then say, "Hey, I don't want to be a downer. After all, this is your party, and we're here to have fun." Then ask him a question. "How were the hors d'oeuvres? Are there any left?" At that point you can move on, and so can he.

## Precept #7: Don't make it smell like bullshit

Never, ever make it sound like an excuse. It's not. It's your reason. After all, it's not your fault. Life got in the way. You have a responsibility to yourself and your receivers to make sure that everyone sees it your way and only your way.

Make sure your words don't fall into the depths of dung despair. Follow the first six precepts of Prophasis: keep it simple, make it feel real, make sure your peeps understand it, invoke sympathy and empathy, don't give too much detail, and change the subject quickly (don't linger). Most importantly, don't distract from your bullshit by whining and bellowing about it - attempting to make sure your words stay front and center for more than the appropriate time is the #1 way to make it look like the crap it is.

With everything good that gets discussed, I would be remiss not to talk about the other items that were found in my cursory research of Prophasis, which I have labeled "Principles and Pitfalls." They are the items that if used correctly can help your cause and if used inappropriately, can hurt.

## The Cross-Examination Conundrum

The first principle and pitfall is the cross-examination conundrum. This conundrum occurs when you get so involved in the goodness of the crap you just delivered that you want to provide more and step in the pile that you made. Not good.

A cross-examination conundrum is where you could get tripped up. You will learn that your excuse needs to get the message across without wasting a lot of time. Your job is to prevent this conundrum like the plague. So, pinch the bullshit out as if it were a fine spice and move on. Don't waste time, words, actions or energy to embellish your words and never, ever clog the drain with too much BS.

Honestly, why open yourself up to more questions?

This reminds me of the story of a friend I'll call "Jim." Jim was weaving quite a tale together about why he didn't stop at the store for some groceries for his girlfriend (yes, he just forgot). He leveraged the traditional travel deflection of, "There was police tape around the store blocking the entrance. I couldn't stop. I haven't seen that many lights in a long time."

Jim's delivery was simple at best. But he made one error – he gave his girlfriend something to worry about and allowed the story to continue.

His girlfriend became physically concerned and while reaching for her purse queried, "Was everyone okay?"

Jim responded, "I think so…" then he remembered that his girlfriend's best friend worked at the store. *UGH!*

"Turn on the news," she replied.

Jim fumbled with the remote, and even applied a little sarcasm by using it as a makeshift microphone. "This is Jim from news channel 5 reporting at the grocery store on third. As you can see, the cop cars are away from the store entrance; they were only blocking the driveways, no ambulances or anything… they have caught a bad driver."

His girlfriend was not amused. She was anxious past the point of listening because her best friend worked at the store. "I better call Viv to make sure she is okay," were her last words.

I don't have to tell you how this all turned out – I think you know. But I can tell you the moral of this story is to not continue slinging your crap because it might just hit you.

### **The Guilt Apothegm**

Another big principle and pitfall that improves or impedes even the best bullshitter is she doesn't use guilt appropriately or correctly - and she should! It's true; everyone says they can use guilt though most don't use it well at all. Most of the time you don't connect the receiver's guilt in his/her mind, heart and soul to what you said, and things go awry. The bad news is that when the guilt train leaves the tracks, there is no coming back from it.

**Despite this, guilt *is* a useful emotion when used on others to achieve your desired results.**

The good news is that if you follow the original seven precepts of the bullprint, you shouldn't have to invoke guilt in the receivers at all. The better news is that when you do use it (given that it is used sparingly), the desired results will be obtained quickly and easily.

Keep in mind and be warned that the potency of the action diminishes by the total number of uses of guilt attempted (especially on the same person).

For example: the receiver will furrow their eyebrows in one of those *are you serious?* kind of looks, and when that happens, be ready to turn on the guilt. It's okay to press that emotional button – remember, you're not pressing yours, you're pressing the receiver's. The result should prevent the receiver from wanting to ask more questions.

As you know, questions can lead to more issues, and that's not good when all you want to do is toss out your excuse and move on. This is where it's handy to have the ability to cry on demand. It works. And if you can't cry, it's always good to say, "I'm so upset I could just cry." For some reason unbeknownst to me, crying has the capability to amplify the guilt in others.

Guilt works best when you can bring up an experience in which the receiver has questioned you, and you were able to prove him wrong, or he has done the same thing as you are about to do and it worked for him. The best example is when you can dig up something from the receiver's past that creates a feeling of personal shame and disappointment in his mind. THIS ACTION IS GUILT GOLD!

The guilt apothegm works well when you know something about the receiver that can be used to highlight your cause, such as the time she brought a cake to work when you were on a diet and how miserable you felt because you couldn't partake in the cake eating with everyone else. The receiver will feel guilty about the incident and not question you further on the current situation.

### The Reverse Apology Juxtaposition

I strained (no pun intended) with this particular area, because it isn't a principle, meaning that you don't have to do it all of the time, and it's not a pitfall per se (unless overused). But it is worth including in the book because it allows your excuse to be wiped clean from the receiver's memory, especially if the subject of your deflection is someone else.

So, what is the Reverse Apology Juxtaposition? It means that if you combine this particular type of apology to your work of art, it will give the illusion of apologizing.

**The trick is, the apology isn't on your behalf; it's in the name of the subject of your bullshit.**

For example, sticking with the dog excuse: "I'm so sorry that crazy driver hit that poor dog," or, "I'm so sorry, I don't know why people are so rude and don't think of anyone but themselves."

It could be a sick kid excuse: "Jimmy feels awful that he is making me stay home with him today. He wants to make you some fridge art." See how the apology isn't for your actions, but rather for someone else you had no control over. And you've done nothing wrong. No blame can be placed on you. This is truly brilliant.

## The Time Disintegration

I will not lie to you, no matter what bullshit you are cooking up, the amount of time you require to develop and deliver your brilliance works against you. Yep, the adage of "shit or get off the pot" is all about making sure you deliver your excuse with a good push of commitment and enthusiasm in a timely manner.

Believe me, I have been there. I became distracted while driving because I was looking at the sights and didn't realize I had missed my turn-off. I didn't realize (before my family did) that we were essentially lost. I lost time in creating and perfecting my excuse because I wasn't aware. In other words, I was too busy doing something else to bullshit. I chose to ignore the circumstances, and voilà; I began to be judged by others (my family) when things went wrong (we got lost). I didn't want the consequences, but I just didn't listen to what my mind had to say to prevent it.

## Sarcasm Neutralization Effect

Another no-no that will allow others to discover you are playing in your poo is by being sarcastic in your delivery. Sarcasm is strictly a pitfall because it gives an emotional trigger in the receiver to stop listening. It creates a moment within the listener's mind to allow her to start analyzing what you have said and why you have said it. The Sarcasm Neutralization Effect can effectively reverse all of the work that you put into creating the original piece of *Connerie*[5], which, of course, isn't what you want at all.

**Sarcasm should be kept where it belongs: for zingers and for the embarrassment of friends and family.**

Mixing sarcasm and bullshit is a recipe for an avalanche that can bury you.

## When it all goes wrong

There is a cautionary tale I need to share. It's of the 35-year-old who was headed down the road of bullshit perfection. Everything was going according to plan, and she was executing the seven precepts of Prophasis perfectly and correctly (or, as I joked, "Prophasis produces perfect poo

---

[5] *Connerie* is French bullshit

pity."). Her reason for not getting what she promised to get done was the best: "My cat is throwing up and I need to run her to the neighborhood vet. My boyfriend will never buy me irises again."

Let's match this excuse to the precepts:

Precept #1:  Keep it simple - Very simple, wouldn't you say?

Precept #2:  Keep it real - Who hasn't experienced a beloved animal throwing up?

Precept #3:  Make sure your peeps understand - She knew the other cat lovers on her team would agree.

Precept #4:  Invoke sympathy and empathy - No one wants their pets to suffer; pets are family. She knew that, and so did the receiver.

Precept #5:  Don't give too much detail - Might have a problem with the word "neighborhood," but in this case all was okay.

Precept #6:  Change the subject - The iris route was brilliant, since they are highly poisonous to cats.

Precept #7:  Don't make it sound like bullshit - This is as real as it gets.

The problem occurred when she called the office for the second time during the day, and she had the need to apply what I call the "Pile-On Permeation." She spoke of the details of the kitty, what happened, the color of the flowers, and how mad she was at the boyfriend, and continued to the point where her friends at work offered to come to the vet to help figure it out.

And guess what happened next?

She started backpedaling to avoid a bullshit collision with the real facts (which is always a disaster). She attempted to cut the call short but she was too late. It fell apart. People wanted to visit her at the vet - they had experienced the same problem but the vet's actions were totally different - and they saw through her excuse. Each of the seven precepts fell by the wayside with a big plopping sound as her bullshit got flushed in their minds. Everything she was attempting to get off her plate came right back on, and with a resounding thud! Sadly, she even tried to employ the guilt apothegm. "Remember when your little munchkin got hurt?" But it was too late; no guilt was going to sidetrack this conversation. By compounding the excuses, she opened up the door to allow the receiver to disengage.

Take it from me: don't listen to your own bullshit to the point where you want to hear more of it. Throw it, let it stick with the help of the No Trouble Bullprint and make a difference in your workload.

Want all of Prophasis' precepts, principles and pitfalls in one handy-dandy little chart? Just can't wait to get your own copy of the No Trouble Bullprint? Just follow the link and I will send it straight to your email inbox for free:

www.BSBrilliance.com/BSB-2

# Chapter Six:
# Many Paths To Bullshit Brilliance

Now it's time to create the strategy for how to effectively deploy the crap. Because knowing what bullshit is… well, that's one thing; but knowing how to fling it is another.

It's time to start replying with the best answer for why you did or didn't do something. And let's get this straight: it isn't about just answering with a "yes" or "no," it's about providing a response that society expects and accepts. It's time to live up to their expectations.

For example: "No, I didn't do it; I watched the game instead," will not do. You want to remove that work from your to-do list, not just leave it on the docket.

**The goal is to protect you AND avoid the consequences.**

It's also not about putting it off until next time. The required result is never to do it nor be asked to do so again. (If you wanted to do it, you would've done it the first time.)

The good news is that there are two, yep, a deuce of different pots to take crap from to create the proper excuse. Both containers will help you generate the best results so that your receivers will not see your actions as fear avoidance, laziness, lack of belief, procrastination, ability challenging, deflection, negativity shielding or a victim mentality.

The first way is Organic Bullshit and the second is Manufactured Bullshit. The biggest difference between these two types is that Organic leverages the *fight, flight or freeze* response to create the deflection, and Manufactured leverages the mind to create the excuse.

**Organic Bullshit**

Organic Bullshit is a part of the God-given design to help create an excuse based on how your body reacts to things. It all starts with the limbic part of the brain, which controls your *fight, flight or freeze* response. If you don't know about the limbic part of the brain, here is a brief description:

- The limbic or mammalian brain controls behavioral memories from positive and negative experiences, emotion, reflexes from a *fight, flight or freeze* response, and value judgments. There are three major areas of the limbic brain: the hippocampus, the hypothalamus and the amygdala.

- The hippocampi (you have two) deal with a consolidation of information from the short-term memory to long-term memory and spatial navigation. (This part of the brain is required for asking directions; maybe I don't have two?)

- The hypothalamus connects the nervous system to the drugstore (better known as the endocrine system) via the pituitary gland. Why is this important? Who doesn't want to know how to get to Walgreens? Actually, the drugstore is what allows the all-powerful meds – endorphins, adrenaline, etc. - to get released into the bloodstream. This helps you react, fast! And fast is what you need to be brilliant.

What I have found is that this *fight, flight or freeze* response gives you access to some awesome bullshit, especially if you understand the circumstances of why it happens to you, *before it actually happens.* In other words, Organic Bullshit leverages the possible symptoms of your body to form perfect excuses so you can miss your committed activities. Other natural areas are stress and sickness! Who is going to argue either? Being overwhelmed creates an awesome signpost to direct you in creating some of the best crap the world has ever seen. Listen to your mind, body and spirit, so you have the time to produce the appropriate excuse and get what you want - absolutely nothing to do.

Here are some examples:

*"I couldn't do anything but just stare, because there was a lion in my car."* (A true excuse told to a colleague of mine.)
*"My heart is racing from almost getting into a fight to protect this girl at school."*
*"I thought I heard someone breaking into my house, so I grabbed my keys and got in the car. I'm at Starbucks attempting to calm down. I'm too scared to go back inside to get dressed."*
*"I am overwhelmed."*

## Manufactured Bullshit

By now we can all agree that poor excuses are the devil's brew, but great crap creation is God's gift. It's a little dramatic but accurate. So, if organic bullshit is the excuse generator of the body, manufactured bullshit is the excuse generator of the mind. Manufactured bullshit consists of excuses flowing in their most fluid state. It can touch everything and everyone without much effort, and actually, if done correctly, will get you sent home without repercussions.

From my informal studies, I learned that people work harder creating bullshit than doing the work itself. Seems appropriate. And if you are putting in the time, shouldn't the excuse be top-notch and amazing? Unless, of course, you have an excellent reason why it's not.

Manufactured bullshit makes you feel good, and, when delivered correctly, helps the receiver out too. These types of excuses are the pile-high barriers required to block the view of receivers, so no one's the wiser when you don't complete the work you promised. They help you preserve your time and energy for the other activities that you want to accomplish such as catching up on sleep, movies, video games, cute cat videos and so on.

**A delivered, accepted, and believed excuse only does one thing: it judges you not guilty of what you didn't do.**

At the end of any successfully delivered bullshit, the undone task remains just as you left it, and hopefully, if the rules are followed, assigned to someone else by the time you get back; and that, my friends, is a thing of beauty. And if you get dirty looks from the person it's been assigned to, don't worry, because they're just jealous that their crap wasn't as good as yours (you should probably buy them a copy of this book to smooth things over).

A big caution: if you use that same good excuse all the time you are going to be in trouble.

For example: you have a large project due at work. You have brilliantly crafted your excuse. Let's say it is the standard: your dog passed away and the family is heartbroken. You use the No Trouble Bullprint to obtain the desired results, and your boss accepts, sympathizes and reassigns your project. He cherishes you as a dedicated soul that cares, and doesn't even connect you with not getting your job done. As time goes on, he recalls you as a fantastic employee and he gives you more responsibility. So you execute another excuse at the opportune time. But instead of going through the process and finding an original one, you leverage the same one again - another animal, a beloved kitty, dies this time. Because of the construct repetition, even if it is true in your mind, by using the same structure, subject and idea you are headed down the path of invoking Prophasis' Law of Diminishing Returns. (It's also a principle and pitfall):

**The success of the bullshit will diminish in direct correlation to the number of times that the structures or subjects are used.**

### REALIZATION RATIO = SUBJECT ÷ STRUCTURE ÷ TIMES USED

So, if you use it once, there is an excellent chance for high success. If you use it many times, the chance of success declines.

Just like any manufacturing process, when you get it right, you want it to keep producing; you will want nothing to change, and you want it to continue providing dividends for you. It is the Henry Ford model of bullshit creation; the receiver can have any excuse he wants, as long as it is black. You want to stick with the same words for all your deflection needs, no matter what. I get that, and it exposes a problem of diminishing returns because science has proven that as you repeat your justification, the amount of effort, self-belief and believability declines. The spirit in which it was intended to be given is removed, and your bullshit doesn't hold up to the wear and tear that was required.

Honestly, to have a consistent go-to defense is a mistake, because switching shit subjects matters.

So, before I go any further, it is time to give you another discovery by Prophasis that I located within some shady archives. This idea is what I have labeled the "Minimum Maxim":

**Make every piece of bullshit different in design, purpose, subject and structure to ensure that you never lose potency because of overuse. In other words, never shit in the same way or in the same place twice!**

And to help you be different every time, I have combed through my notes and found the acronym JUDGE to help you remember that you have choices.

Now for a quick view of what is coming: JUDGE represents the five important diversified classifications of bullshit; each needs to be structured in their own way and leveraged in the right circumstances if you want the desired results. JUDGE stands for Justification, Ugliness, Defensiveness, Gratification and Entitlement. It contains a plethora of material so you can create some of the best crap in the house, maybe in the state, probably in the country, and, if you bullshit extraordinarily well, in the universe!

You, too, can have a personal copy of the "JUDGE ME NOT GUILTY" cheat sheet that gives you the basics of what each type of bullshit can provide. Just follow the link and I will send the gift straight to your email inbox for free:

www.BSBrilliance.com/BSB-3

# Chapter Seven:
# Justification Bullshit

*Justification [juhs-tuh-fi-kay-shuhn] n: something such as a fact or circumstance that shows an action to be reasonable or necessary; a statement in explanation of some action or belief; the act of defending or explaining or making excuses for by reasoning.*

What a fantastic introduction – thank you, free online dictionary/thesaurus. There is no doubt that the Justification bullshit is rich in nutrients as we attempt to protect ourselves from the world with the minimal amount of effort.

As you can imagine, there is a significant amount of poop that one can conjure up to protect one from the outside world. Each nugget seems to fall into one of four important categories: Time, Energy, Terminating and Obstructing.

## Time Bullshit

Time is the biggest and best piece of crap that we have because everyone can identify with it. Everyone is stressed, overworked and underpaid. Everyone is attempting to fit one more thing into his or her day. And everyone totally understands when the next drop in the glass will cause it to overflow. It seems Time is the "go-to" manufactured excuse everyone will appreciate, because they are out of time, too.

> *"I didn't have enough."*
> *"I had too much."*
> *"There aren't enough hours in the day!"*
> *"I need more."*
> *"Where would I fit this in my busy day?"*

A word of caution: keep in mind the Minimum Maxim. Because of its popularity, time is also the most overused pieces of shit there is. If this is your only selection from what I'm going to share, you will wear down the acceptance and believability quickly.

**I like to say, save "time" for when you need a surefire winner, and only dump on others at that moment.**

This excuse tends to leak and fail when the receiver's argument in return is, "Where did all of your time go?" She knows that there are 10,080 minutes to use in a given week, and you have given her a chance to wonder what you did with yours.

Sure, you will attempt to quickly figure out that your weekly allotment of time falls into broad categories of sleeping, eating, bathing/dressing, relaxing, improving, working, playing and schooling. Though, if pressed by the receiver, there will be gaps, and these spaces create conversational pitfalls and cross-examination conundrums, because you can't explain where the time you had went!

So, if you're going to use time as your excuse, be sure that you have done all of the calculations beforehand and deliver it in one breath. My reasoning is that it doesn't give your receiver a chance to question any of it; she will surely get bored with the amount of detail and will just walk away. For example:

*"Well, actually I CAN account for every second since I spoke to you last week. I spent 3.7 minutes each of the 14 times brushing my teeth. Then there was the one and a half hours getting ready each morning – including the typical showering, morning constitutional, ironing, dressing, and feeding my dog. I then spent 30 minutes to make and eat breakfast, and make my lunch, which by the way, someone normally steals from the fridge, which caused me to have to go out to eat three times for about an hour a day. Then, on most days, I spent 38 minutes driving to my office. Did I tell you about the two accidents this week that caused more than a 50-minute delay each time? Of*

*course, I am at work for at least 50 hours a week. The pressures of work and home are giving me less than the optimal eight hours of sleep. There was also my one date night that I had in the last three months for two hours and uhm. . . 15 minutes. I went for a confessional at the church for about 66 minutes. It appears there was a lot to talk about, if you know what I mean. Dinner preparation and eating was a whopping one hour a day. I should probably slow down cause eating fast makes me feel gassy and bloated. Don't you hate that feeling? Which reminds me: it got so bad I had to go to the doctor and that was 30 minutes, AND he was an hour late! He was a gastroenterologist and urologist and I had to tell him about the 53 trips to the bathroom this week. Anyway, after adding up all the times I needed to go potty, I spent 8.5 minutes on average on that cold hard seat. Oh, of course can't forget the traveling to him and coming directly back to work, which was a total of 45 minutes. I watch TV or read a book for about one hour each night. There is also the shopping, getting gas, having my car washed after the mudslides, and had to buy new tires – that was a total of 3 hours. Laundry, evening shower, dishes, dog walks, yelling at the neighborhood kids, and catching up on current events were a total of 5 hours. And not to mention the 5.2 hours on my damn taxes. . . which reminds me I have to cut this short because I have to file them before midnight!"*

It is important that you convert your receiver from the notion that you had time and show her that you had no time. Also note that the receiver will use the amount of available time since she asked you to accomplish the task or job - so be prepared; don't get caught in your crap trap! And take care of your health. I think it's clear that bullshitting well takes a lot out of you!

**Energy Bullshit**

There's nothing like harnessing the steaming power that bullshit can create. For centuries, it was burnt for heat and fuel. Today is no different, though now it is used for a higher purpose. Honestly, this is my second favorite excuse next to "time," because chances are it is true, not only for you but for the receiver (at least at some time in his life). There are periods when you are tired, overworked, unbalanced, and are giving everything you have in life to whatever cause you are choosing to focus your energies on at any given moment (or at least you have given that impression). And your receiver knows that when you hit these moments, even thinking and planning is not on the schedule.

*"I am already giving a hundred and ten percent."*

*"I can't do any more."*

*"I'm at my max."*

*"I'm too tired."*

*"I'm brain-dead."*

*"I don't have enough brainpower left to give."*

For example: you show your parents how unreasonable the teacher is being by giving you enough homework to last a lifetime – except you must complete it all in a day, and you have five teachers all doing the same thing. How can they pressure you like that? You conveniently leave out that you've had the syllabus for a month (especially if you retain Prophasis' precept #5).

In the work environment it's old hat; there's nothing easier than to tell your boss that you are at your max. You don't have to offer solutions (unless you're asked), you don't give facts or data, and you look pissed off or surprised that he could add one more straw to the camel's back.

Two nuggets of caution: One, don't ever say anything about someone else having more energy, because that comparison can haunt you when the receiver responds with a comment about how much you get paid. Two, the mistake that I often see when energy is used as the deflection is when you have documented history of doing anything else within three days of the due date (think Facebook, Instagram, Twitter). Bad idea, so don't document what you do if it is going to disprove your poo.

One last note: It is crucial that if you use Energy bullshit, your body language will need to match what you are saying. You can't be upbeat and tell a depleted energy story. The receiver will figure it out. Make sure your body language matches what the receiver is about to hear. When the receiver buys it, you don't have to stay late or come in early. *(See the Prophasis' Positional Prescription in the next chapter for more help.)*

**Terminating bullshit**

Terminating phrases have the effect of stopping the receiver from asking more questions. They frequently contain the words "can't," "won't," and "don't." By using these words to lead the bullshit, you will set limits to your abilities and leave the impression that nothing can get you over the hump to accomplish whatever it is you said you'd do.

*"I can't do it."*

*"I can't be responsible..."*

*"I won't be coming in today because... "*

*"I won't do that."*

*"I don't know how."*

*"I don't have the skills."*

Probably one of the biggest benefits of terminating excuses is that the receiver will retain and recall that you shy away from things. He will remember how you wriggled and squirmed around the requirements and that you are scared of your own shadow. The receiver now knows that you aren't willing to go figure it out, which means that he will not ask you to do it again. AWESOME! Finally, a payoff for <u>not</u> knowing something. How many times does that happen? Exactly. Well done.

**Obstructing Bullshit**

This type of bullshit (sounds painful - don't worry, no laxative needed) allows you to throw a wrench into the gears of progress. You can use these ripe nuggets to set the stage of possible delays to get to your boss's final goal. In other words, you need more time before you can dump the results on her desk. This category tends to include the words "shouldn't," "didn't," "haven't," "wouldn't," "couldn't," "isn't" and "wasn't."

> *"I shouldn't go out tonight."*
> *"I didn't break the machine."*
> *"I haven't decided yet."*
> *"I couldn't do that."*
> *"I wasn't in charge."*

Most obstructing excuses are there to slow down the delivery of what you promised to accomplish, but they tend not to remove it. These are great if your goal is to buy time or if you're attempting to stretch out a job and make more money by taking longer to get it done than you promised. They also work if you want to have some fun, catch some rays, go to Vegas or help your friend get (or get over) a hangover.

# Chapter Eight:
# Ugliness Bullshit

A strange name for a not-so-strange kind of crap. This category allows us to convert the input from your five senses into a bullshit-shooting Gatling gun. Yes, it starts with what you see, hear, touch, taste and smell, but it's not the first action or sensory input that you are after. It's all about how you could interpret and use them so that others believe that you can't continue what you are doing.

The brilliance of using any of the senses is that others see, hear, touch, taste and smell the same things you do. And if the receiver is also affected by it, then you have some good shit!

Think back to when you were a kid and mom served liver and onions: you had an adverse reaction, brought it to mom and dad's attention (probably through whining, crying and complaining about the smell), and your parents made you something else to eat. Why? They know the scent was foul and the food tasted bad. The benefit is the parent now understands that you have an issue with this food. Mom or dad probably had the same reaction when he or she was your age, and parents don't want their kid to repeat their mistake. So they let you off the hook.

Now, as I promised in the previous chapter: there is a principle and pitfall that Prophasis specifically calls out for "ugly" excuses - Prophasis' Positional Prescription – and it states:

***Most bullshit delivered needs to have the correct body language and inflection of voice to achieve success.***

Without employing the Prescription consistently, the wrong gestures or inflections will dislodge the sympathy (Precept #4) from taking hold.

We were great at this when we were kids and wanted to avoid school. We would pretend to our moms that we didn't feel well with that nasal quality, fake coughing, etc. We understood at that young age how important it was to make our sound and facial expression congruent with our words!

The value of Prophasis' Positional Prescription is that it reminds you that even successful bullshit derails when the entire mind, body and spirit are not in tune with their desired results.

**Hearing Bullshit**

Hearing excuses are normally small, probably well-meaning statements, each one easily becoming deflections of why you didn't do something. It should be based on what others don't hear as well. A word of caution: if there are others in the room and you are the only one with the excuse on why you didn't hear something, then it is probably you vs. them, and it will fail.

You can also use the old standby of pretending not to hear what the speaker is saying as a deflection to give yourself some time to create an even better bullshit response.

*"I wasn't listening."*
*"I couldn't hear you."*
*"I thought you said…"*
*"I thought you heard…"*
*"Your voice is so high pitched."*
*"You spoke so low."*
*"I don't/didn't understand what you said."*
*"They talked too fast."*
*"They sounded funny/annoying."*

## Smell Bullshit

"It didn't smell good (and basically this type of bullshit never does), so it made me wave my hands, and that knocked that bowl of hot soup on you. It's the soup's fault for not smelling good." (Stop laughing.) Are you saying that never happens? It does! The world labels them as accidents.

Recall Prophasis' Positional Prescription when delivering this type of excuse by asking yourself how you might respond when different types of chemicals give off a pungent odor.

*"It/they/he/she smells/stinks."*
*"I don't want to eat it because of the odor." (Usually said while holding one's nose.)*

## Touch Bullshit

"Ugh, gross! I'm not touching that!"

Slimy, icky, and sticky all come to mind. There isn't anything even close to your fingers, but you can mentally feel it; you almost don't want to touch the next page of the book (I promise it will have only theoretical bullshit on its pages). You are probably thinking up some good reasons not to have to touch it (especially if you don't want to continue reading). Yuck to the touch of paper. What are we, savages? If it's not digital, it's gross.

For example: It's a hot summer day, 110° in the shade and you feel the sweat under your arms. Your hair sticks to your head, and the sweat dribbles onto your forehead. Your toes are even sticking together (this is any summer day in Phoenix). The worst part? You still have two hours before you're done working. Honestly, does that make you want to complete your goal, or maybe put it off for another day because tomorrow may be cooler?

*"It's slimy."*
*"Too slippery... I couldn't get a grip."*
*"I am dripping wet; I need to go home and change."*

**Taste Bullshit**

Sweet, salty, sour and bitter. Sounds like an old guy attempting to impress his caregiver at the old folks' home or a candy salesman – your choice, same bullshit.

This crap is leveraging four of the five regions on the tongue that provide you the necessary input to determine how something tastes. Apparently, after eating it you're supposed to give it the fairest of shakes as you decide if you like it. Yeah, right. Recollect when mom told you to eat that stuff on the fork? Well, if you had some knowledge of what it would taste like, this bullshit would work every time.

Don't make the mistake of limiting it to just taste - it can also be how it feels in your mouth (the textural sensations), or issues with it going down (e.g., a small esophagus). It can also be how it makes you feel after you have eaten it (e.g., it gives you gas, the squirts, or, my favorite, it makes you bloated.) Leverage everything you can if you want to taste the success of great bullshit.

> *"I don't like the taste."*
> *"It's too sweet/salty/bitter."*
> *"It makes me want to puke."*
> *"It gives me gas."*
> *"It's overwhelming to my senses."*

Oftentimes you are aided from some of the other senses like smell, sight and touch. You will even be able to recall distant memories ("My mom used to make me eat it as a kid!") to help create an excuse that is hard to argue. Everyone has an issue with something, why not you?

Let's go back to the plate of liver and onions and apply Prophasis' Positional Prescription:

You know it looks and tastes like crap. But if you smile, voice your opinion in a monotone way, and look directly in your parents' faces while saying you don't like it, it won't have the appropriate response, and no one is going to believe that you won't be eating it. Now, if you scrunch up your face, hold your nose, look away, change your voice to be whiny, and toss in a few dry heaves I bet that the appropriate response to your bullshit is within your grasp.

The Positional Prescription is displayed in front of the receiver, which of course tends to cause the receiver to have a stronger memory of this instance than most other bullshit you could use. So it will be imperative to do the same thing, the same way, with the same subject – or it will fail.

A word of caution: This is one category that purposely violates the Minimum Maxim. You shouldn't change your likes and dislikes at the drop of a hat. You need to be consistent with them: every time liver and onions gets served, you need to have a similar reaction as the first time you used the excuse.

## Visual Bullshit

This area is problematic because it allows your loves, likes, prejudices and hates to creep in. "Those kind of people took up too much of the lane at the checkout line and I couldn't get through to get to the exit" just allows too much data to be in the hands of the receiver. Honestly, it gives your receiver too much data about yourself - and that is the last thing you want to do. If I rank all of the bullshit that you can use, Visual should be on the bottom. It just gives too much personal information away.

> *"They're slobs."*
> *"They're too fat/skinny."*
> *"I can't take a chance to get what they have."*
> *"They disgust me."*

There is one method that flies against my warning, and that is if the subject of the bullshit is considered a criminal. Then I find that this works perfectly. For example: "I was at the grocery store and the three little hoodlums that walked in looked like they were going to cause trouble, so I left to get help."

Though there is a saving grace to this crappy subcategory. Prophasis gives this little nugget:

**Don't aim your crap at a person as much as a thing.**

In other words, let your subject be inanimate. For example: *"The building didn't look safe enough to enter."*

# Chapter Nine:
# Defensive Bullshit

This category is almost too easy to write because most of us have practiced it throughout our teenage years. Yes, defensive bullshit isn't new, but it needs to be mentioned because this one grouping tends to lead you down a path that violates some of the precepts, principles, and pitfalls, especially the cross-examination conundrum and the pile-on permeation. Why? Because the receiver wants to get to the "bottom of the situation," so she'll prolong the conversation. Of course, this means the longer the conversation, the more chances that she will see through your crap. *UGH.*

**And as you have learned, you don't want more questions, you want less.**

You don't care what the root of the matter is because all you want to do is get away from spending any more time on the current tasks.

This category requires the receiver and speaker to be engaged in a conversation before delivering the bullshit. Also, it is worth noting that you should not hold your ground and stay looking at the receiver; walking away in a huff is not an option but rather a requirement (keep in mind precept #4 and #6) for the full effect to be felt by the receiver.

The defensiveness category includes three essential areas: Deflect, Detour and Delay. Each can generate a whopper amount of crap all in the name of you not doing what you are supposed to do - how can you not love that! I won't waste any time; let's get right into it.

**Deflect Bullshit**

Your dad asks, "Did you have fun last night?" You take it to mean, "I know what you did," so you react and respond with, "What, are going to watch me every second of the day?!"

That, my friend, is one form of defensive *rahat*[6], when another person has communicated with you and you leverage this opportunity to respond as if you were verbally attacked. The goal of deflection BS is to make sure that you have invoked the Guilt Apothegm within your receiver. You don't want to take any chances that he won't be sympathetic to your cause.

---

[6] *Rahat* is Romanian bullshit

Now, there is a big difference between using this as a teen and as an adult. As a teen (especially before you read this handy-dandy book), chances are you're feeling guilty about the subject, and self-directed guilt is a bad idea. Your brain has given you the immediate protection of a snotty retort (which, by the way, didn't work, and now your parents know that something else went on; this is the perfect example of the Sarcasm Neutralization Effect harming you). That, or you think there is some holier-than-thou perceived expectation of you and you don't know how to handle the disconnect between what you did and what Dad wanted, so you just carry on hoping to wear him down (which never actually happens – remember, he taught you how to bullshit).

As an adult, you want to leverage a deflection without the internal guilt; you don't want the receiver to leverage what you say to obtain more detail, but you do want the desired results of removing the task or activity from your to-do list. So, here are some handy-dandy "bullshit bullets" for when to best deliver defensive bullshit that no one will want to step near. Use deflect bullshit when:

> **Deflection Bullshit Bullets**
>
> 1. The receiver is knowingly being accusatory (or even just when you think what they just said can be taken as accusatory).
>
> 2. The receiver is visibly upset at you.
>
> 3. The receiver's question to you is a known hot button.

*"I can't believe that you brought that up."*
*"What did you mean by that?"*
*"Are you going to watch me every second of the day?"*
*"Jimmy (or any co-worker) doesn't do it, why should I?"*

## Detour Bullshit

I would like to introduce to you two of the best words that have caused their fair share of getting you to avoid responsibility for your actions. Both words negate what a person just said; I call them phrase erasers. They are useful when you want to sound confident, but you have an alternative crappy intent. Welcome to the wonderful world of "but" and "however." Here is how I suggest you squeeze this bullshit in to a conversation:

**Put a positive statement at the front and the excuse at the end, separated by one of the two words, "but" or "however."**

Why? Because everybody likes to hear good things about themselves. And by using a positive statement, it opens a critical door to the impending deflection to be retained.

For example:

*"I always wanted to be a guitar player like Eddie too! However, it's more important to me to be a great father."*

*"I so appreciate everything you do for me. But, I won't be able to help you move today."*

There is no doubt that how you structure your bullshit matters; it needs to stand firm so that it takes root into the awesome fertile soil called the receiver's mind. So, here are some helpful steps to leveraging this subcategory into a thing of beauty.

## **Detour Bullshit Bullets**

1. Pick a positive statement - it's best if it's about the receiver. This opens the receiver's mind for acceptance.

2. Pick your favorite phrase eraser - "but" or "however" (and it's a lot of fun when you use them both - "But, however, like I was saying . . .").

3. Insert your bullshit. Evoke precepts 1, 2 and 3: keep it simple, keep it real and make sure your peeps will understand.

4. Deliver it with a positive and forward-thinking attitude in mind. As far as the receiver thinks, everything you say smells like roses.

5. Even though this advice flies in the face of Prophasis' Positional Prescription, you have to deliver your crap with all of the positiveness in step #1.

## Delay Bullshit

You will be happy to know that there is another set of words that can protect your right to not do a darn thing. These words are the ones that help you delay the activities that you are attempting to do, but, for whatever reason, are not excited about doing. Think of these phrases as preemptive bullshit that you will plant so that when things don't work out, you've got something to fall back on and repair the situation. Most receivers, I've found, don't even process these as an excuse or deflection until it's been too long for them to do anything about it. In fact, many feel these are entirely acceptable.

These words are "try," "maybe," "I'll see" and "I know."

Let's start with "try." "Try" doesn't indicate that you will or will not do anything; it's saying that you *might* attempt it. Try implies thought but little or no action. Trying gives you permission to fail in your task without responsibility. In fact, by using "try," you are setting up a likely answer when the receiver requests why it didn't happen. "I will try my best" has so many outs that it becomes a very popular response from many speakers. The coolest thing is that agreeing to try isn't even a commitment. And yes, Master Yoda[7] was wrong: trying is fine if you aren't planning on doing what you said in the first place and you're just looking for a way not to hurt someone's feelings.

"Maybe" and "I'll see" are cut from the same cloth. They both present the easy road: the one that carries you away from what they want you to accomplish. Think of the times when you have used either of these when asked, "Can you?"

Someone asks, "Can you do this for me?"

You reply, "I'll see." Hmm… Is that a yes or a no?

Mom asks, "Can you take out the trash?"

You respond, "Maybe." Now mom doesn't know if the garbage will go out.

Both of these phrases are nothing more than delaying your real answer of "no," and I suspect you're hoping they will forget.

---

[7] Star Wars Episode V: The Empire Strikes Back – Master Yoda said, "*Do or do not. There is no try.*" (But, he is still wrong.)

That leaves "I know." This phrase is solid bullshit because if someone points out something that you need to improve upon or change, a response of "I know" puts an end to the discussion. What more can a person tell you if you already know?

Be extra careful with the "I know" phrase, because it can doom you. When you use the "I know" deflection to get out of responsibility, you are now taking full accountability for your knowledge because you've said, "I know." You have been warned (Yes, I'm aware you know).

Don't tell anyone, but my business partner Jeff and I used to tell people "How to succeed without trying." If you want to check it out, just follow the link and I will send it to your email inbox for free:

www.BSBrilliance.com/BSB-4

# Chapter Ten:
# Gratification Bullshit

Gotta love it.

Gotta want it.

Gotta have it.

Gotta be easy.

Now, before we go any further, I have to set the record straight. I am not talking about the *long-term, take forever, look back over a life and be proud of what happened* type of gratification.

The relish of past experiences should be reserved for wedding anniversaries, birthdays, pep talks, retirement parties and funerals. Because, unless you miss the event (and if you do, you'd better have some awesome BS prepared), this type of crap is an example story exaggeration and credential adaptation bullshit that I described at the beginning of the book.

But there are things to learn from long-term gratification that need to be discussed.

First, it can be a fertile training ground for practicing your short-term science. It gives you a chance to get used to delivering your message to a crowd and learning how to pull at those heartstrings.

Second, it allows you to select words and phrases that match the theme, mood and energy of the environment. This bull poopy works really successfully because most don't remember or care about what is being said during the moment as long as the feeling is appropriate, and it helps the receivers of the bull to have the expected emotional response - be it to laugh, sigh or cry.

Third, it lets you have some fun and make that crap connection for someone of need.

Though as you know, I'm not here to talk about the long-term, no siree, Bob! I am only talking about the short-term deflection-dung variety of gratification. The instant type of gratification that society bombards you with on a day in, day out basis on TV, billboards and even at home. Yep, the instant coffee kind, where you expect the best, but don't have the time to wait for it. The kind that if it takes too long you are willing to leave it on the counter. The type where the steps to make it aren't to your benefit even if it takes mere moments. And yes, sometimes measuring is too big of a chore in the moment to get that hot beverage for your spouse, so forget about the coffee and go for a side of bullshit.

Don't get me wrong, there's nothing incorrect with wanting something in the shortest time possible, wanting it with the least amount of effort, or wanting it at a particularly high standard. But who wants to be forced to deliver it to someone else like that?

This is why gratification bullshit works so well, because most receivers want the same thing. They are asking you to do something because they want it now, they want it easy, and they want it their way – they just don't want to do it.

The key to this deflection is to catch the need for instant gratification early: if you perceive that it's not going to be easy, now, and your way, then it is time to prepare your poo for the receiver.

Prophasis introduces a very special principle and pitfall for this category: It's called the Fulfillment Formulation, which states:

**It's not about you; it's about them.**

So, keep this in mind if you are using this type of crafty crap to get yourself out of trouble:

---

**Gratification Bullshit Bullets**

1. Your instant gratification needs to be grounded in the receiver's activity, not yours. It needs to be something the receiver has to do for you.

2. The receiver must be perceived at fault.

3. The Guilt Apothegm needs to be applied, hard. Your plans have to be changed or stopped because he/she hasn't gotten something to you. (The horror, the shame!)

---

What I have found is that a gratification excuse isn't about speeding up the receiver to deliver (keep in mind, your intent is not to do the work), it is saying that since the receiver hasn't given it yet, you are moving on, skipping, removing, and avoiding his/her task.

The goal of this bullshit is to show the receiver that because he can't, won't or couldn't get what you needed quick enough, you will have to do something else. He is welcome to call you later (if he can find you), he can put it back on the schedule (if it isn't already full of other BS), or, the best answer, he can assign it to someone else.

A word of caution: if you have any notion that the receiver may not believe you, don't hesitate to season your bullshit with a smidge of guilt. You also have the option to compound this excuse with another reason (yep, this is the one case where the pile-on permeation works in your favor).

Infuse your bullshit with something along the lines of, "My word means everything to me, and I just get so upset when anyone questions my integrity because it's all I've got." Or how about the ever-popular psychologically turbulent alternative, "I guess it's all my fault. I can never do anything right. My life is one terrible mistake." Or the simple but effective, "Yeah, I suck!" All will get a response and usually in your favor. But, like with all bullshit brilliance, don't overuse it because it will lose its effectiveness.

*"I can't be expected to do everything."*

*"If no one wants to help me, then why should I do anything about it?"*

*"Look, if it was important, why didn't you do it?"*

*"I'm the only one who does anything around here, and the first time I run out of time it's the end of the world."*

*"Do you know how long I've worked here? I deserve a break . . . I've given this place the best years of my life."*

*"My get up and go has got up and went."*

*"If only I'd had more to drink, maybe I'd actually be able to finish."*

*"There's nothing more pathetic than being nagged."*

*"How can I get it done if you keep bugging me?"*

*"If I made the money you make, I'd have had it done by now."*

# Chapter Eleven:
# Entitlement Bullshit

I've left this for last, because, well, for one thing, it is the E in JUDGE, and second, it is all because this one is about YOU.

An entitlement deflection is all about how age, race, creed, gender, religion, sex, tenure, level, bank account, position, experience or education (to name a few) makes you exempt from having to do the work.

This awesome category of fertile material comes into play because you will use the result of comparing what, how, who, why, and when you do something to/for someone else. It then takes that pain and anguish that would be mentally, physically, emotionally, and spiritually created and turns it into the required outcome that will allow others to judge you not guilty.

Once again: it is all about you, and nothing else matters but you. About time, right?

Yet most don't ever use this emotionally charged category of amazing deflection material. Why?

Mostly because it's not politically correct, it makes people uncomfortable, and it's not appropriate in all group settings.

Fortunately, there are four other great letters in the JUDGE fecal material that can produce the results you are looking for. But the best reason I have seen why people don't use entitlement: it doesn't matter to them and they are not going to be stopped from achieving their goals (even if bumps, bruises, wounds, exhaustion and exile are the result) and my hat would be off to them, if it weren't so hot today.

But why use this amazing bucket of E-shit? You have personal material that could be used to shake, rattle and roll the receiver's mind. You have control over a vast richness of words and phrases that you can bring to any conversation because of this category.

Honestly, why would you let what you compare yourself to hold you down? Why not use it to your advantage? And that is where this bullshit comes in. It deals with creating excuses when you want others to believe there is some overriding privilege that you can invoke to remove the work.

Now, out of all of the bullshit in this book, this should be used the least.

Because if you keep playing the same record over and over, you will invoke Prophasis' law of diminishing returns. It will become less useful for you. It also has another pitfall: entitlement has the biggest backlash for the long term.

Because it gives your receiver more information than he deserves. Every entitlement excuse leaves a little piece of your internal mental workings as a weapon to be used against you at some point in the future - and no one wants that! So please, use it sparingly.

Here are the most popular excuses that come from entitlement:

*"I deserve it."*
*"I have already put in my time."*
*"They have deprived me; it's only fair."*
*"I don't want to work for it."*
*"Me first."*
*"I'm too old/young."*
*"My upbringing says I don't have to do that."*
*"I have too much/little education to achieve it."*
*"I make too much or not enough."*

You've gotta practice what you preach. And to help you out, I have put together a fill-in-the-blank bulls**t generator game that might just give you the needed help to improve your art. Heck, you can even play this with your friends. Just follow the link and I will send it straight to your email inbox for free:

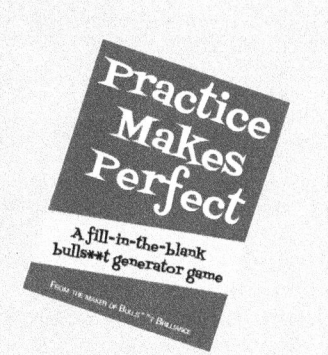

www.BSBrilliance.com/BSB-5

# Chapter Twelve:
# Real Examples of Bullshit Brilliance

This bullshit thing is easy-peasy once you get the hang of it. To make my case, I thought it would be a blast to provide you with your personal starter kit: think of it as potty training wheels. I've written a couple of scenarios and included some of the great bullshit I might use. In the blank spaces, write what you would use.

**You are late to an event and you need to tell your boss why.**

1. Blame someone else or some other event without it looking like you're blaming them. For example, say something such as, "I know some people are irresponsible and don't care about others, but it doesn't give them the right to drive like idiots. And if it weren't for them I'd have been here on time. Let's forget about them and have some adult beverages."

2. "The neighbor's car broke down, and she was crying, and so I had to jump-start her car. Her husband should do a better job of maintaining their vehicles." Then

quickly ask a question, not related to being late but about the receiver of the excuse. Now the subject is changed and he is distracted. Simply genius.

3. "I said I would "try" to get here on time… it just didn't work out."

4. _____
_____
_____
_____
_____
_____
_____
_____
_____
_____
_____
_____
_____
_____
_____
_____
_____

**You told your spouse that you'd clean the house over the weekend and you didn't do it.**

1. When the spouse gets home and the house is a mess, but dinner is on the table, you can easily justify the dirty rooms by stating how hard you worked on making the perfect meal. You can also talk about spending a long time at the grocery store getting all the ingredients to have a beautiful feast together because nothing is more important than family. Boom. Can't argue with that one. As long as that meal isn't two cans of chili simmering in a pot, this excuse works great. It redirects her disappointment from what wasn't done to how well what did get done was done. Of course, have her favorite adult beverage ready and waiting. Also, make sure to get her eating dinner right away, and then ask about her day. Once you get the subject changed, you're in the clear.

2. The spouse gets home, the house is a mess and there's no dinner on the table. The laundry is in the same place on the floor. In fact, there are even more dirty dishes in the sink. It takes a particular kind of bullshit to get through this scenario unscathed. "Sorry, honey,

I went to get started on the yard early and was moving the tools when I threw out my back. I kept going because I knew that you'd be disappointed if I didn't get it all done. The truth is, I've been in so much pain that I could hardly move." It's tough to argue back pain. Then finish with a flourish: "I'm so sorry that I'm not as strong as you and couldn't fight through the pain to get it all done. I promise to do it next week."

3. _____
_____
_____
_____
_____
_____
_____
_____
_____
_____
_____
_____
_____
_____
_____

# Chapter Thirteen:

# Better Bullshit Than The Bullshitter That Is Bullshitting You

I have no doubt that bullshitting will continue to take its rightful place in the world. And one of the downfalls of more people using it is that at some point in the near future they will send their crap in your general direction to avoid the commitments they have made to you.

Let's talk about how to not only spot a bullshitter, but also derail his poo from getting near you or on you. I use the following three steps to bullshit the bullshitter: Recognition, Derailment and Injection.

**Recognize Bullshit When You See It**

The #1 item for dealing with the BS from another is recognizing that it is bullshit in the first place. Of course, the better the speaker, the more obscure the crap. So you are going to have to dig deep in the pile of poo to figure out what it really is. I won't lie to you, the more practice that the speaker has, the more he believes his crap doesn't stink.

I know that most think that a bullshitter can't be BS'ed. Well, that's just not true; from my limited studies, I find that 62.9% of bullshitters get crapped on just like anyone else. Actually, some believe their own shit so much that, in essence, they crap themselves. But let's just concentrate on the people that are attempting to poop on our parade.

Your ability to not fall into their pile of dung is 100% related to identifying and controlling the situation as fast as you possible can. So listen closely to everyone and trust no one. You need to watch for their avoidance of the consequences through the telling of their story, which means first you need to figure out what they're attempting to avoid.

**Look not at what they're talking about directly, but what they're trying to distract you from seeing.**

The speaker is using manure manipulation to sidetrack the conversation to make him feel not guilty of his actions or inactions. You have to be aware if you want to identify any type of bull that is thrown in your general direction. The speaker wants you to look away long enough for him to get away.

> **Recognizing and Identifying the Bullshitter**
>
> - He should be avoiding absolute answers if they relate to "yes" and "no" questions.
>
> - He will have a tendency (and, if he has read this book, the requirement) to change the subject as fast as he can.
>
> - He will avoid the Cross-Examination Conundrum like the plague. He wants nothing to do with facts (real or imagined) because it will give too many openings to derail his story.
>
> - He will turn on the guilt and won't turn it off.

## Derailing the Crap Caboose

Now that you have identified and recognized that he is on the train, it's time to derail his crap caboose from the tracks before he gets the results he desires. But before I tell you how to accomplish it, I want to tell you what not to do.

Definitely don't call him on it, especially if you are planning on bullshitting back, because if you do, he will know that consequences are coming, and a fertilizer fight will entail. See, at the moment that he realizes he has been caught, the bullshitter will hunker down and pucker up to protect himself. He will employ the deadly Accusatory Annihilation Algorithm (AAA) to recapture the conversation because it is going south.

The AAA process works like this: The speaker angrily blames someone or something else at the moment that he believes his original deflections aren't working and he might be caught. (This is deflection BS and a pile-on permeation rolled up into one nicely executed pile of doo-doo.)

For example: in the political world when the going gets tough and the world isn't believing what he said, the Accusatory Annihilation Algorithm will be employed. Yes, the bullshitter who is in trouble will throw someone else under the outhouse.

So, what should you do?

There are four qualities that allow you to derail your friendly deflector:

> **Derail The Deflector**
>
> 1. Let him feel comfortable flapping around in his pile
> 2. Look for ways he can self-derail
> 3. Have fun
> 4. Waste his time

To achieve all four, I employ what I affectionately call the Continuation Corollary, which in essence tells you to suspend your disbelief and play along with the speaker by giving him the impression that you believe everything he says.

Waste his time by leveraging the time disintegration principle that I talked about in a previous chapter, which has been proven mentally fatal to a BS'er, enjoy the crap-fest by helping his story grow past containment, and look for the opportunity to kick his caboose squarely off the track. The cross-examination conundrum becomes the perfect weapon for pushing the poo-choo train off the rails – quietly.

**By continuing the story rather than fighting it, you will create plenty of openings for your questions to not be answered.**

It is always best if the bullshitter goes away on his/her own.

Maybe an example would help explain this:

I get calls from overseas Windows support, a lot. They always tell me the same thing: "Your Windows PC has a virus." I know they are working hard at their ruse, so I play along. I go to great lengths to help their story along while collecting data on how I will be derailing the conversation; sometimes I keep them talking for 20 minutes. I pretend to tap on my keyboard, I ask them if the virus gives the blue screen of death or if it locks up the machine. I work hard in leveraging their own conversation against them while pretending that I believe what they say. I ask them for specifics of what they see. I ask them if they are seeing the same thing on their side (which they always say "yes".) I let them talk and continue to tell their story, because I know the truth – I don't have a virus, because I don't use Windows. It never fails; they will hang up long before I am done.

## Injection of Better Bullshit

Now, for what you have been waiting for. Here is an opportunity to upstage the bullshitter attempting to bullshit you. Yep, you are going to bury her in her own bullshit, because everything she said can now be used against her. You will need three things to make this happen: the opening, a shovel and the plug.

The opening is an opportunity to take control over the conversation. Though this can be done a myriad of ways, here are my two favorites:

1) Attempt to one-up the story by telling another story. You want to make sure that your bullshit has a similar subject to what the original bullshitter was saying. If not, it will give a clear indication that you are bullshitting him. From my example: "I remember the virus of 2008; it was a disaster to my company… "

2) Use the reverse apology juxtaposition to your advantage - except this time, you and the original BS'er are the subjects of the apology. This allows for what our Greek goddess called a boring, yet effective,

bridge. For example, using the PC BS from above, "I am so sorry that the virus in my machine has affected you. I'm sure you have better things to do with your time…"

I suspect by now you know exactly what you need to do to shovel the bullshit on top of them. You've got it: leverage the entire No Trouble Bullprint with all of Prophasis' precepts and principles to construct and deliver brilliant crap that this world has ever seen. Just to remind you:

> Precept #1: Keep it simple
> Precept #2: Keep it real
> Precept #3: Make sure your peeps understand
> Precept #4: Invoke sympathy and empathy
> Precept #5: Don't give too much detail
> Precept #6: Change the subject
> Precept #7: Don't make it sound like bullshit

Don't make the same mistake the original bullshitter made - don't waste time playing in your crap. Get in, get out and leave him wondering how he stepped in his own steaming pile.

Now for the pièce de résistance: the plug.

After you have Recognized, Derailed and Injected your own brand of bull, you now need to stop him from spewing his crap in your yard ever again; it's very simple.

Call him out – straight faced (even if you are laughing on the inside), stern looked (don't even crack a smile), move a little closer (if you move away he will disconnect from the emotional hook that you are creating), bring your hands together and fidget with them (like you are creating an evil plan), and say the words, "And never attempt that again."

Then walk away. Don't fall into the trap of saying anything else. Let the originator be scared, frightened, or wondering what will happen next. Let your words stew in his mind. And the best part is that every time he sees you, all you have to do is stare at him and all of the emotional feelings will come gushing out all over again.

Though there is one caveat: make sure he is capable of handling the mental and physical anguish of the plug, because it will stretch his psyche and screw with his head. And your goal is not to break him, which might cause unexpected damage; your goal is just to stop him from bullshitting you ever again.

# Chapter Fourteen:
# Never Deliver Borderline Bullshit

Well, you have read how to make your shit shine better than everyone else's.

You know exactly what you need to do to make sure that you can avoid the commitments that you made to others. Sure, your deflection could affect your family, friends or even your boss, but you know that it is better to let them down easy than just to miss the obligation all together. And if you have leveraged all of the manure in this manual, they will appreciate the amazing skill that you have used so you don't have to do the work. They will give you your final marks on successfully implementing the teachings in this tome - if they only knew you used it.

Yet, with all of the knowledge, with all of the thousands and thousands of words that have come before this, you have decided not to take this advice to construct and deliver the brilliance you have been trained to do. You took the easy way out. You didn't go all in on your bullshit delivery. You decided to walk the line between doing what you promised and getting out of it for good.

Let me give you a visual. You are attempting to keep one foot on the dock of deflection and one foot on the boat of commitment, and guess what ... YOU FAILED. All that happened was that you fell into Liability Lake. Now you are going to be thrashing and splashing around in the cold water, attempting to keep afloat, finding yourself exhausted and not becoming brilliant in either world. *UGH*.

So do yourself a favor: Decide.

Decide to take the easy way out, or, if you want to do the work, decide on doing what you promised. Decide with your feet, mind, body and spirit to either put them on the boat of commitment or leave them on the dock of deflection.

Let me tell you Larry's story to help:

> *It was a night like every other night, one where the moon rose as the sun settled down for its regular nap. This evening, a simple request came across our hero Larry's phone, "Tomorrow is the big day...everything is riding on it... One more presentation and we have the contract."*

*Larry studied it, even scrolled to read the other texts from the boss that were delivered this week. Each one attempted to pump him up, each adding more work to his evening, and each taking time away from what he wanted to do. Larry knew that the boss didn't want to deliver it himself; there was too much on the line and he would be under a lot of pressure. It was a life or death contract. Larry wallowed in the facts that he created about how they were taking advantage of him. They were setting him up. Larry just knew that his boss was transferring the responsibility to his lonely shoulders, so he would be a fall guy.*

*Larry needed to make a decision. He needed to be committed to his plan. His dad's voice could be heard in his mind, "If you are going to do something, do it right." So, Larry did the right thing for him, he wrote his boss back, "Between sneezing and coughing, I've been going through it . . . but the drugs are making me drowsy."*

*The boss wrote back, "Get some sleep."*

*Larry was happy because that was the message that he hoped for, one of empathy and sympathy. Larry didn't rest on his laurels; he checked Facebook to see what everyone else was doing that night. He posted for help, "Quick Flu Remedies? ANYONE?"*

*Larry watched TV and caught the cliffhanger to his favorite show. He delivered a couple of texts with the same sick information to other people at work. He even had a couple of visitors from the upstairs apartment with their hometown remedy, beer. He used his presentation as a coaster. Larry even went to the local bar, though he was smart: "No photographs!" he shouted. Everyone laughed.*

*It was after midnight by the time he got back to the house. He still had time to get a full read in, but because of his commitment to his brilliance, he found less and less need to actually accomplish it. So, as he was getting ready for bed, he wrote his boss one last time, "I will be there at 8 a.m. but I think I am going to bring a bucket with me." And by the time his head was hitting the pillow the boss wrote back, "Ugh... just stay home; I guess I'll deliver it." Larry was very pleased at the sparkling shit he had just created.*

*By the following nightfall, the chips had fallen; he heard the news from his boss's boss that the presentation had been a disaster, they had lost the contract and they had fired his boss. Oh, and the big boss was offering Larry a promotion.*

*The moral of Larry's story: Good things can happen when you "decide" to play with brilliant bullshit.*

Regardless of which you choose, put your effort and energy toward getting it done brilliantly. The time spent won't be wasted; sure, one of the ways will keep you safely in the world you know and the other will take you on a trip of a lifetime, but who needs real-life adventure when there's TV? Who needs to meet new people when you're just going to have to train them in accepting your bullshit as if it were all true? Who needs the pressure of actually getting the real work done appropriately or dealing with the fallout if you don't, especially when you don't ever have to do it in the first place? Isn't that success?

When in doubt, just consider the words of Prophasis:

***Kateplikse tous me labres malakies i apla spatala hrono ke kane tin doulia, i epilogi ine diki sou.***

Or if your *greeklish* still isn't top-notch...

***Bedazzle them with Brilliant Bullshit or just waste the time and do the work, your choice.***

Well, you are done with your training and you deserve congratulations! You are now eligible for a Bachelor of Science in Bullshit Brilliance (or as I like to say, "a BS in BS"). Just answer a couple of questions to test your bullshit brilliance knowledge and your official personalized Diploma will be yours. Just follow the link and take the "final". If you pass with flying bulls**t colors (mostly natural browns), I will send your diploma to your email inbox:

www.BSBrilliance.com/BSB-Complete

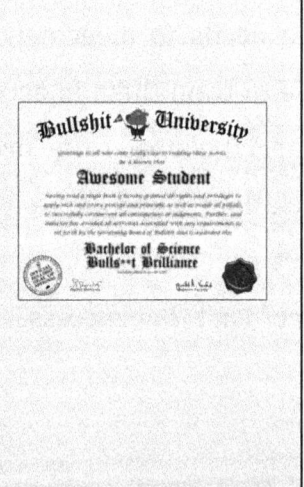

# Final Thoughts:
# Sometimes *Skitsnack* Is Just *Paskapuhe*[8]

Why in the world would I write this book?

In my experience, I found that every "how-to" book written (e.g., "Take action") can also be seen as a "how not to" book (e.g., "How not to take action"). Any time positive rules are given they also provide the space for the opposite to be discovered.

For example - though I don't condone inappropriate drug use – "Don't do Drugs" policy manuals give you the rules and regulations, but they also make you aware of the loopholes that are available. School handbooks make it clear what is black and white, which means everything that isn't in the rules is considered gray and okay. And even the dictionary is used as a loophole because of the absolute definition of a word ("is" is now a presidential defense).

The problem is, it just takes too long to decipher the gray

---

[8] *Skitsnack* is Swedish bullshit and *Paskapuhe* is Finnish bullshit

areas and read between the lines. So, I leveraged what I saw people doing over five decades of life experience in an attempt to expose the gray, with the hope that they would see for themselves what they are doing to themselves.

My hope was that by writing about "how to use bullshit" readers will read between the lines for "how NOT to use excuses," because, in the end, excuses get you nowhere fast. They make you feel good for a moment, but hurt you in the long run.

At the end (and this *is* the end of the book), there isn't a word, phrase or action that removes the responsibilities from what you did or didn't do. **It's your fault**. I firmly suggest that you just answer with "Yes, I did" or "No, I didn't," take your consequences, and keep moving forward. It might make others mad because you have broken the social convention of not giving the rest of the story, and you're not making up the bullshit that they want to hear.

It will be worth it because you will start figuring out pretty quickly that when you remove the excuse and flush the crap away from you, you increase your personal productivity and start getting what you want.

What I found really interesting during the research of this book was that bullshit in a few other languages tended to translate into very interesting and telling words:

- Garbage *(Belarusian)*
- Blah *(Bengali)*
- Nonsense *(Bulgarian, Chinese, Hungarian, Javanese, Korean, Lithuanian)*
- Vomit *(Esperanto)*
- Ravings *(Estonian)*
- Prank *(Filipino)*
- Folly *(Georgian)*
- Rubbish *(Hindi)*
- "It deceives" *(Kyrgyz)*
- "This hooliganism" *(Malagasy)*
- "But the facts" *(Marathi)*

It appears that many languages around the world know that bullshit is nothing more than empty space. So in the immortal words of myself:

> **Actions speak volumes; words say nothing, and bullshit is just empty words.**

Do yourself a favor and remove excuses from your existence. Instead, concentrate on conditioning the mind, body and spirit to accomplish what you want. Make sure that any perceptions and expectations that are set are the ones you set for yourself. You need not give up any responsibilities to motivate yourself, because it all falls on your shoulders. A lack of motivation means one thing: you have chosen to be lazy. Being lazy will not make your dreams come true. Period.

But if you have to use bullshit because the commitments that you have made are just too much to handle, please fling yours better than any monkey at the zoo, because you have now been properly trained. You're welcome.

And above all, be brilliant in all you do!

> If bullshit isn't your thing, how about reading about how to NOT let excuses get in your way? My business partner Jeff and I have authored a small book called "Between Do & Done Is What You'll Become" to help you on your way. Just follow the link and I will send it straight to your email inbox for free:
>
> www.BSBrilliance.com/BSB-Bonus

# About The Author

Joel S. Levinson knows what it is like to walk to the abyss, get sucked in, make excuses, stare his future self in the eye and pull himself back out. He has experienced wild success as a five-time serial entrepreneur achieving multi-millions in revenue and has been President of multiple $100M business units in the Fortune 500. Yet he also is intimately familiar with failure - almost losing himself, his financial freedom and even his connection to family and friends.

Today he applies his expertise and energy to create a movement for ambitious men and women to have a meaningful and fulfilling life beyond their comfort zone. Having been nearly crushed by life's responsibilities - financial bankruptcy, family tragedies and health concerns - his zest for learning, acceptance of change and positive outlook are the keys to his success. He leverages his talents, acquired knowledge and hard-earned wisdom to help others avoid the pitfalls that nearly did him in. His techniques and skills help those who want more out of life step out of the rat race that prevents real success and join their inner being with their outer doing to reach their dreams.

Co-author of the book "Live The Risk: Escape your excuses and enjoy life," Co-host of "Live The Risk presents Walking With Warriors" podcast, the soon-to-be-released "Jeff and Joel Show," and the co-creator of the Live The Risk company, he is a consummate catalyst for generating actions that accelerate positive results in his clients' lives.

Joel is humbled to be the dad of two beautiful daughters, Jaime and Sarah. And he is blessed beyond belief for the 32 years (and counting!) of marriage with his bride, Jackie. His family is his life.

**Other books by Joel:**
Live The Risk: Escape your excuses and enjoy life
Miss You: A gift from mom
The Defenders of SMASH: A martial arts adventure story

**Other published works:**
Send an email, Save a Life (chapter)
AWARE (chapter)
Do and Done (Magazine article)

# About Live The Risk

The Live The Risk company was created to help ambitious individuals break free of their comfort zones by helping them visualize success, understand obstacles, remove excuses, take action, and build habits to achieve their goals and dreams. Joel Levinson and his business partner, Jeff Steele, are also considered the leading experts in rental property prosperity. www.LiveTheRisk.com

## About The Jeff and Joel Show

Jeff and Joel are in the midst of creating a video internet show to help support and encourage their viewers to take control over their time and life. www.JeffandJoelShow.com

## About Wealth Through Rentals

Wealth Through Rentals is leveraging Jeff's more than 20+ years of real estate rental success and Joel's 30 years of business knowledge to help their tribe find, fund and buy rental properties that will activate their wealth and life by using passive income. www.WealthThroughRentals.com

www.ingramcontent.com/pod-product-compliance
Lightning Source LLC
Chambersburg PA
CBHW071517040426
42444CB00008B/1690